About this book

The General Strike 1926 has been described as the most important event in British politics between the two World Wars. The dramatic pictures in this book trace the events of those momentous nine days.

The author shows how the General Strike grew out of the bitter quarrel over pay and working conditions between the miners and mine-owners; how the other unions joined in; how the Government organized volunteers to run essential services; and how, in the end, the miners lost and had to return to work on lower wages and longer working hours. The popular picture of the strike is of Oxford undergraduates loading and unloading goods, society ladies peeling potatoes, and titled gentlemen driving engines. All this did happen, but the pictures also show the other side of the story — the sheer desperation of people living and working in intolerable conditions who felt they had to express their frustration in some way.

AN EYEWITNESS HISTORY BOOK

Wayland

The General Strike

Anne Mountfield

More Eyewitness History Books

The Age of Drake
Animals in War
Beads, Barter and Bullion
The Changing Seaside
Children of the Industrial Revolution
Clothes in History
Country Life in the Middle Ages
The Firefighters
Florence Nightingale
The Glorious Age of Charles II
Greek Myth and Legend
The Horseless Carriage
Islam
Kitchens and Cooking
Livingstone in Africa
Markets and Fairs
The Mayflower Pilgrims
Men in the Air
The Monarchy
Newgate to Tyburn
Overland to the West
Pirates and Buccaneers
The Police
Popular Entertainment

The Printer and his Craft
The Railway Builders
Road Transport
Roman Roads
Shakespeare and his Theatre
Ships and Seafarers
Shops and Shopping
The Slave Trade
Sport through the Ages
Stagecoach and Highwayman
Steam Engines
The Story of the Cinema
The Story of the Wheel
Street Cries
1066
Tom-tom to Television
The Tower of London
Toys in History
The Tudor Family
Tutankhamun's Egypt
A Victorian Sunday
When Dinosaurs Ruled
Witchcraft and Magic

Frontispiece: Lines of strike-bound buses in London during the General Strike.

First published in 1980 by
Wayland Publishers Ltd
49 Lansdowne Place, Hove
East Sussex BN3 1HF, England

ISBN 0 85340 765 7

Phototypeset by Trident Graphics Limited
Reigate, Surrey, England
Printed and bound in Great Britain
at The Pitman Press, Bath

Contents

1 'A Fit Country for Heroes'

November 11th 1918 saw the end of the First World War. The soldiers returned from the muddy trenches of France and Belgium. Nothing seemed too good for them. The Prime Minister, Lloyd George, promised to make Britain 'a fit country for heroes to live in'. But it did not turn out like that.

In the years before the Great War the gap between employers and employees was greater than it is now. For half a century, trade unions had been growing. Workers had come to see that they were stronger if they stood together against their employers. They were finding that to go on strike and refuse to work could be an effective weapon.

All over Europe, things changed after the war. Kings and Emperors were overthrown in Russia and Germany. In many countries there were strikes and street fighting between communists and fascists. In Britain, things were calmer. There was no revolution, but there were many strikes in 1919 and 1920.

Most of the strikes in Britain were in protest against unemployment, low wages, and poor working conditions. In 1919 both the police and railway workers went on strike. There were many local strikes in the coal mines, and a national one in 1920. Miners' wages rose when coal prices were high and fell when trade was bad which resulted in great hardship for miners and their families. In 1921 there was a big coal 'lock-out', when the men refused to accept a cut in wages. The miners hoped for help from the railwaymen and transport workers. But in the end they had to fight on their own, and lost. Five years later they were to fight again in the General Strike.

THE GREAT WAR These soldiers are knee-deep in the mud of a First World War battlefield in France. Nearly all fit men under the age of forty-one had fought in the war. By the time it ended in November 1918, three-quarters of a million British soldiers had died. The men who came back from the trenches expected life to be better than before the war.

THE KHAKI ELECTION After all they had gone through during the war, people wanted peace and the hope of a better future. There was a General Election in December 1918: it was called the Khaki Election because so many voters were still in uniform. Lloyd George, the Prime Minister, promised 'a fit country fit for heroes to live in . . .'

REVOLUTION IN EUROPE The war had made many countries restless. In Russia the Tsar had been executed after the communist revolution in 1917. The picture shows Russian Cossacks brandishing their swords at a demonstration in Petrograd, 1917. After Germany was defeated in 1918, the German Emperor was overthrown, and a communist revolution nearly succeeded there too. In many countries there were strikes, and fierce riots between communist and anti-communist political parties.

HITLER AND THE NAZIS   In Germany unrest led to street battles between socialists, communists and the Nazis — a new party led by Adolf Hitler. The picture shows an artist's impression of Hitler addressing a meeting of the German Workers' Party (Nazis). In 1923, Hitler tried to start a revolution in Munich in southern Germany. It failed, and he was sent to prison.

BRITAIN'S FIRST LABOUR GOVERNMENT The British socialists — the Labour Party — wanted to take power by winning an election not by fighting a revolution. In January 1924 they came to power when the Conservative Government lost a vote of confidence in the House of Commons, and the first Labour Government was set up. Ramsey MacDonald was the Prime Minister. He is the man with the moustache in the centre of the front row in this picture of the cabinet. But the new government only lasted a few months. The Conservatives won a new election in November 1924.

STRIKES IN BRITAIN People were restless in Britain, too. In 1919 there was unrest in the mines, and a railway strike. There was even a police strike, which led to looting of shops in Liverpool. This picture shows London policemen on strike. They were striking for the right to be allowed to belong to a trade union.

OUT OF WORK At first men returning from the trenches had little trouble finding work. But then trade hit bad times. By the middle of 1921, two million people were out of work. In some towns, half the men had no jobs. The unemployed men opposite are carrying poppy wreaths on Remembrance Sunday 1921. The first Sunday in each November had been set aside to remember the war dead. They are also carrying banners demanding work. Below, jobless men queue at the Labour Exchange.

ALL RIGHT FOR SOME Life for the rich quickly got back to normal after the war. Motor cars were becoming common. Women's skirts were getting

shorter. Life doesn't look too bad for these ladies on their way to an Agricultural Show at Tunbridge Wells in the summer of 1921.

'KING COAL' Coal mining was Britain's biggest industry. If pit wheels like this one stopped, the things that depended on coal stopped too — trains, factories, power stations and warm homes. Over one million men worked in the pits — four times as many miners as there are now. They dug 250 million tons of coal a year — well over twice as much as now, and 100 million tons of it was exported. They called it 'King Coal'.

WORKING UNDERGROUND This picture shows
the hard, dirty work underground. Nowadays coal is
cut by great machines. Then it was dug out by hand,
with a pick-axe, by men working in the narrow seam
of coal. Often the seam was only a metre thick.
These men have no safety helmets, and their lanterns
hang from the pit-props.

PIT DISASTERS Coal mining has always been dangerous. Sometimes the roof collapses, and miners are buried under tons of rock, or cut off without air. Another great danger is explosion; coal gives off a gas, which may collect in the narrow tunnels and can

easily be set off by a spark. This picture shows miners' wives and families waiting at the pithead for
news of their relatives after a disaster. The horse-
drawn ambulances are bringing bodies up from the pit.
Over 1,000 men were killed in the pits every year.

MINERS' HOMES Life was hard for miners' families too. They usually lived near the pit in rows of terrace houses like these, 'two rooms up and two down'. Often there were no baths at the pit and no bathrooms in the houses. The miners had to clean up in a tin bath in front of the fire. You can see opposite that the open fire was used for boiling kettles of water.

THE MINERS' LOCK-OUT, 1921 This man is urging miners in Wigan to hold out against wage cuts. In 1921 the export price of coal fell to less than a quarter of what it had been in 1920 which meant that miners' wages fell. During the war, the Government had run the mines. In March 1921 it handed them back — with all their problems — to the owners. The mine-owners decided that they had to cut back on wages. The miners said no. So the owners locked the miners out of the pits — a strike in reverse.

BLACK FRIDAY, 1921 Before the war, the miners had made an alliance with the railway workers and the transport workers in which they agreed to stand together in a strike. This was known as the 'Triple Alliance'. The miners hoped the other unions would help them fight the lock-out. But on 15th April 1921, the other unions called off their support. The miners called it 'Black Friday', and in the end they had to go back to work for lower wages. Here, Frank Hodges, one of the miners' leaders, arrives for talks at the Board of Trade during the lock-out.

2   The Strike Begins

After their defeat in 1921 the miners went back to work. For a while trade got better, more coal was sold abroad, and wages rose. But then trade fell badly again in 1925. The mine-owners said they could not run their mines at a loss. They tried their only answer – to cut wages again, and make the miners work an extra hour a day. The miners got other unions' help, and threatened a general strike in July 1925.

The Prime Minister, Stanley Baldwin, realized that the Government was not ready to face up to a general strike. So he set up a Commission under Sir Herbert Samuel, to see what should be done. Meanwhile the Government paid the mine-owners a grant so as to put off a cut in the miners' wages. In that way, Baldwin gained time. He used the breathing space to make careful plans to fight a general strike.

And in May 1926, a general strike was called. When Samuel's Commission made its report, the owners and the miners could not reach agreement on a wages cut. The miners had support from all the other trade unions. The Trades Union Congress (T.U.C.) met at the end of April, and on Saturday 1st May they called a general strike to start the next Monday, 3rd May 1926.

So the first General Strike in British history began.

'NOWT DOING' Trade got better in 1923, and miners' wages rose. But in 1925, exports dropped again, and the owners tried to cut wages back once more and add an hour to the working day. The man in a flat cap is the miners' leader, Herbert Smith, who said 'Nowt doing' in response to the mine-owners' proposals. This time the miners stood firm, and the railwaymen and transport workers promised help. A strike was ordered by the union.

RED FRIDAY, 1925 This is the Prime Minister, Stanley Baldwin, arriving at a meeting of owners and miners. He decided something must be done to prevent a general strike. The Government offered the mine-owners a grant of £24 million, so that miners' wages would not fall. Baldwin set up a Royal Commission under Sir Herbert Samuel to see what should be done. The strike was called off on 31st July 1925: this time the miners called it 'Red Friday', to mark their victory.

Organisation for Maintenance of Supplies.

What is the O.M.S. ?

The O.M.S. is an association of loyal citizens organised in the public interest, without political or class partisanship.

What is the Object of the O.M.S. ?

The object of the O.M.S. is to provide the Government in times of emergency with classified lists of those who will assist in maintaining essential public services ; in ensuring the necessary provision of food, water, light, fuel, power and transport to the community, and who, when called upon by the constitutional authority, will co-operate in upholding law and order.

Such co-operation is the natural duty of every citizen, but it can only be effective with organisation. Such organisation is supplied by the O.M.S.

How will the O.M.S. Operate ?

The O.M.S. will not intervene in private or sectional conflicts. It contemplates only lock-outs or strikes of so far-reaching a character as to disorganise the machinery of social life and so to affect the well-being of a community. It in no way impugns the right to strike, and only seeks to prevent the mass of the population being victimised by a conflict for which they are not responsible.

Its activities will be exercised under the control of the constitutional authority by volunteers of British nationality. As soon as normal conditions are restored they will resume their ordinary vocations.

Who will Benefit by the Operation of the O.M.S. ?

The general community, whose vital interests must not be compromised to secure those of a particular section, or for the purpose of promoting political aims.

Who are the Principal Sufferers from an Interruption of Public Services ?

Children, the infirm and the aged. Those who have least resisting power will suffer most, and the disabilities ensuing from suspension of transport and communications will fall most severely on the poorest class of the population.

How can Citizens help the O.M.S. ?

By registering themselves with the committee of their Borough or local area as volunteers to assist according to their several capacities.

By explaining to others the objects of the O.M.S. and encouraging them to register for public service.

What Obligations does a Volunteer incur ?

He signifies his acceptance of the principle on which the O.M.S. is based, viz., that it is the duty of the citizen in times of emergency to co-operate with the Government in maintaining supplies and public services, and he offers his own personal service in the event of his being called upon by the constitutional authority. Such services will be rendered as far as possible in the employment or business in which he is actually engaged.

No levy is demanded from those who register under the O.M.S.

PREPARING FOR THE WORST While the Samuel Commission was at work, the Government made plans to deal with a general strike to ensure that food and other essentials would be kept moving. A private 'Organisation for the Maintenance of Supplies' – the OMS – was set up. It kept lists of people willing to help keep things going if there was a strike. This is one of its leaflets.

THE SAMUEL COMMISSION   This is Sir Herbert Samuel, arriving at a meeting of the Royal Commission on the Coal Industry. The Samuel Commission published its report in March 1926. It proposed some improvements in the miners' working conditions, but it also said that since many pits were making a loss, the miners must agree to lower pay.

THE TRADES UNION CONGRESS The Trades Union Congress joined together all the trade unions, as it does now. The T.U.C. held a special Conference on 29th April 1926. A general strike was called for Monday 3rd May, in support of the miners. The T.U.C. took over control of the strike.

'NOT A PENNY OFF THE PAY' The Government and the owners demanded that the miners agree to pay cuts, and longer working hours. The miners flatly refused. The picture opposite shows the secretary of the miners' union, A. J. Cook. He gave the striking miners their slogan: 'Not a penny off the pay, not a second on the day'.

PLANNING THE STRIKE   Ernest Bevin, on the right of this picture, was the union leader in charge of planning the strike. Unlike the Government the unions had not made detailed plans for a general strike. They decided not to bring all workers out on strike. Besides the miners they planned to call out railway and transport workers, and workers in heavy industry, such as the steel, electricity, gas and building trades.

Trades Union Congress General Council.

THE MINING SITUATION

PROPOSALS FOR CO-ORDINATED ACTION OF TRADE UNIONS.

[It should be understood that memoranda giving detailed instructions will be issued as required.]

1. SCOPE.

The Trades Union Congress General Council and the Miners' Federation of Great Britain having been unable to obtain a satisfactory settlement of the matters in dispute in the coalmining industry, and the Government and the mineowners having forced a lock-out, the General Council, in view of the need for co-ordinated action on the part of affiliated unions in defence of the policy laid down by the General Council of the Trades Union Congress, directs as follows :—

TRADES AND UNDERTAKINGS TO CEASE WORK.

Except as hearinafter provided, the following trades and undertakings shall cease work as and when required by the General Council :—

Transport, including all affiliated unions connected with Transport, i.e., railways, sea transport, docks, wharves, harbours, canals, road transport, railway repair shops and contractors for railways, and all unions connected with the maintenance of, or equipment, manufacturing, repairs, and groundsmen employed in connection with air transport.

Printing Trades, including the Press.

Productive Industries.

(a) **Iron and Steel.**

(b) **Metal and Heavy Chemicals Group.**—Including all metal workers and other workers who are engaged, or may be engaged, in installing alternative plant to take the place of coal.

Building Trade.—All workers engaged on building, except such as are employed definitely on housing and hospital work, together with all workers engaged in the supply of equipment to the building industry, shall cease work.

Electricity and Gas.—The General Council recommend that the Trade Unions connected with the supply of electricity and gas shall co-operate with the object of ceasing to supply power. The Council request that the Executives of the Trade Unions concerned shall meet at once with a view to formulating common policy.

Sanitary Services.—The General Council direct that sanitary services be continued.

LOCAL STRIKE PLANS Each union sent out orders to its local branches, telling them to strike from midnight on Monday 3rd May. Telegrams were sent first, with detailed orders following by letter. Strike committees and Councils of Action were set up all over the country. Meetings were held to decide which workers should strike, and to arrange for pickets of workers outside work-places.

DINNERS 3'6

RESTAURANT

3   The Strikers

The General Strike began at midnight on Monday 3rd May 1926. By the Tuesday morning, workers in transport, printing, heavy industry, and a few others were on strike. The miners themselves were 'locked out' by the owners for refusing to take a cut in wages. There are no exact figures of how many men were on strike or locked out, but it was around 3 to 4 million workers. The T.U.C. had chosen vital groups of workers — especially the railway and transport workers. The country seemed paralysed. Buses and trains stopped running. Newspapers did not appear. In some places the strikers even danced triumphantly in the streets.

As well as supporting the miners, many workers in other trades came out on strike in protest at the high unemployment and low pay in many parts of the country. There was a great feeling of the workers standing together. The miners' job was dirty and dangerous, and many were already living in great poverty. Many workers thought the miners had been treated unfairly by the owners and the Government.

Fortunately, there were few violent incidents during the General Strike. Some buses and trams were overturned, a train was derailed, and a few street fights broke out between strikers and police. But the Army stayed mostly in the background. People had feared that the General Strike might lead to a revolution, like the Russian Revolution in 1917. Instead, many strikers went to church, or played football with the police.

T.U.C. HEADQUARTERS This picture shows the headquarters of the T.U.C. in London at the start of the General Strike. The strike was run from here.

Workers wait in groups, hoping for news. Despatch riders stand by their motor bikes, ready to take secret messages to the various trade unions.

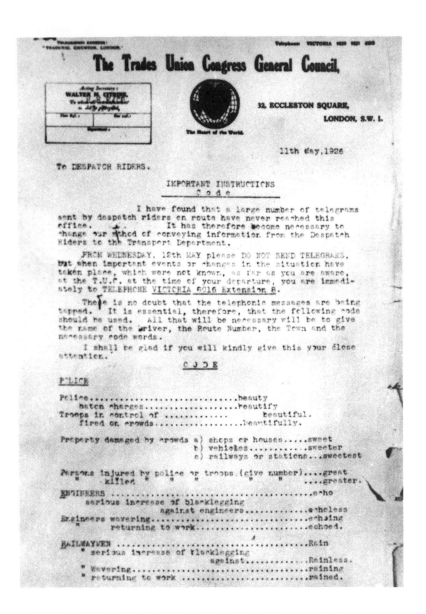

The Trades Union Congress General Council,

32, ECCLESTON SQUARE,
LONDON, S.W. 1.

11th May,1926

To DESPATCH RIDERS.

IMPORTANT INSTRUCTIONS
C o d e

I have found that a large number of telegrams sent by despatch riders en route have never reached this office. It has therefore become necessary to change our method of conveying information from the Despatch Riders to the Transport Department.

FROM WEDNESDAY, 12th MAY please DO NOT SEND TELEGRAMS, but when important events or changes in the situation have taken place, which were not known, as far as you are aware, at the T.U.C. at the time of your departure, you are immediately to TELEPHONE VICTORIA 6016 Extension 8.

There is no doubt that the telephonic messages are being tapped. It is essential, therefore, that the following code should be used. All that will be necessary will be to give the name of the Driver, the Route Number, the Town and the necessary code words.

I shall be glad if you will kindly give this your close attention.

C O D E

POLICE

```
Police...............................beauty
baton charges.......................beautify
Troops in control of ...............  beautiful.
fired on crowds.....................beautifully.

Property damaged by crowds a) shops or houses......sweet
                          b) vehicles............sweeter
                          c) railways or stations...sweetest

Persons injured by police or troops (give number)....great
     "    killed  "    "    "    "    "         ....greater.
ENGINEERS ...........................................echo
    serious increase of blacklegging
                against engineers............echoless
Engineers wavering..............................echoing
    returning to work............................echoed.

RAILWAYMEN ............................................Rain
    serious increase of blacklegging
                against............Rainless.
    "  wavering......................................raining
    "  returning to work ............................rained.
```

MESSAGES IN CODE The T.U.C. needed to send messages all over the country, and get news back about how the strike was going. They thought telegrams were being read by the Government, and telephones tapped. So they worked out a secret code. The picture above shows the instructions given to despatch riders.

STRIKE BULLETINS The T.U.C. ran its own newspaper during the strike – called The *British Worker*. Its job was to keep the strikers in touch with what was happening, and keep their spirits up. It appeared each day, with news about how effective the strike was. Other union bulletins were issued locally. This edition congratulates workers on the splendid response to the strike call.

THE
BRITISH WORKER
OFFICIAL STRIKE NEWS BULLETIN
Published by The General Council of the Trades Union Congress

No. 1.　　WEDNESDAY EVENING, MAY 5, 1926.　　PRICE ONE PENNY

IN LONDON AND THE SOUTH

Splendid Loyalty of Transport Workers

EVERY DOCKER OUT

" London dock workers are absolutely splendid," said an official of the Transport and General Workers' Union.

" So far as they are concerned, it is a 100 per cent. strike. There is no trouble and everything is going smoothly."

POLICE HELP REFUSED

At Swindon, the railwaymen are obeying Mr. Cramp's injunction to remain steady and to preserve order. The Great Western works are, of course, closed, and no trains are running.

It was stated at a mass meeting of the N.U.R. that Mr. Collett (the

The General Council suggests that in all districts where large numbers of workers are idle sports should be organised and entertainments arranged.

This will both keep a number of people busy and provide amusement for many more.

chief mechanical engineer) had declined the offer of the police and the military to guard the railway works, saying he could rely on the strikers to preserve law and order. Railway workshops at Wolverton, Crewe, and elsewhere are closed.

CHANNEL SERVICES

At Dover the tram-ways staff are out. The cross-Channel boat service is greatly curtailed, and a large number of passengers are awaiting the opportunity to cross.

NOT ENOUGH!

From 3¼ to 5 million workers have ceased work.

The Government announced by yesterday's wireless that 30,000 volunteers had registered, expressing willingness to take the strikers' places. It doesn't seem enough!

Published for the General Council of the Trades Union Congress by Victoria House Printing Company, 2, Carmelite-street, London, E.C.4. Telephone (8 lines): 6210 City.

WONDERFUL RESPONSE TO THE CALL

General Council's Message : Stand Firm and Keep Order

The workers' response has exceeded all expectations. The first day of the great General Strike is over. They have manifested their determination and unity to the whole world. They have resolved that the attempt of the mineowners to starve three million men, women and children into submission shall not succeed.

All the essential industries and all the transport services have been brought to a standstill. The only exception is that the distribution of milk and food has been permitted to continue. The Trades Union General Council is not making war on the people. It is anxious that the ordinary members of the public shall not be penalised for the unpatriotic conduct of the mineowners and the Government.

Never have the workers responded with greater enthusiasm to the call of their leaders. The only difficulty that the General Council is experiencing, in fact, is in persuading those workers in the second line of defence to continue at work until the withdrawal of their labour may be needed.

WORKERS' QUIET DIGNITY

The conduct of the trade unionists, too, constitutes a credit to the whole movement. Despite the presence of armed police and the military, the workers have preserved a quiet orderliness and dignity, which the General Council urges them to maintain, even in the face of the temptation and provocation which the Government is placing in their path.

To the unemployed, also, the General Council would address an earnest appeal. In the present fight there are two sides only—the workers on the one hand and those who are against them on the other.

Every unemployed man or woman who " blacklegs " on any job offered by employers or the authorities is merely helping to bring down the standard of living for the workers as a whole, and to create a resultant situation in which the number of unemployed must be greater than ever.

The General Council is confident that the unemployed will realise how closely their interests are involved in a successful issue to the greatest battle ever fought by the workers of the country in the defence of the right to live by work.

MESSAGE TO ALL WORKERS.

The General Council of the Trades Union Congress wishes to emphasise the fact that this is an industrial dispute. It expects every member taking part to be exemplary in his conduct and not to give any opportunity for police interference. The outbreak of any disturbances would be very damaging to the prospects of a successful termination of the dispute.

The Council asks pickets especially to avoid obstruction and to confine themselves strictly to their legitimate duties.

SOUTH WALES IS SOLID !

Not a Wheel Turning in Allied Industries

' MEN ARE SPLENDID !'

Throughout South Wales the stoppage is complete, and everywhere the men are loyally observing the orders of the T.U.C. to refrain from any conduct likely to lead to disturbance.

So unanimous has been the response to the call of the leaders, that not a wheel is turning in the industries affiliated to the T.U.C.

MONMOUTHSHIRE

Complete standstill of industries in the eastern valleys. Absolute unanimity prevails among the rank and file of the affiliated unions, and not a single wheel is turning in the allied industries.

Monmouth Education Authority—which has a majority of Labour representatives—has arranged to feed the school-children where required.

ABERDARE VALLEY

All railway and bus services are at a standstill. The miners' attitude indicates that they are absolutely loyal to the advice of their leaders to refrain from anything in the nature of riotous behaviour.

NEATH

The workers have unanimously responded to the call in support of the miners, and the stoppage is complete.

With one exception, safety men are remaining at their posts.

The behaviour of the men is splendid.

AMMAN VALLEY

Every industry and almost the entire transport services are at a standstill at Ammanford and throughout the populous Amman Valley.

GLAMORGANSHIRE

The men are obeying implicitly the instructions of their leaders not to create any disturbance. Crowded meetings of miners have registered their unanimous intention to stand by the T.U.C.

ABERTRIDWR

At the Windsor Colliery, Abertridwr, a deputation of the men and the management met and agreed to safety men being allowed to work.

A Trades Council, composed solely of branches affiliated to the T.U.C., has been formed to act as a Lock-out Committee for Abertridwr and Senghenydd.

PORT TALBOT

Perfect order is being maintained at Port Talbot, where all the industries are shut down.

41

MASS MEETINGS This is a mass meeting of miners in Durham during the strike. One of the strikers' problems was finding out what was happening. The usual newspapers were stopped, and not everyone

had one of the new 'wireless' sets, which were only just becoming common. One way of keeping people informed was by mass meetings of strikers which were held in many large towns.

'FOOD ONLY' PERMITS   The T.U.C. had decided before the strike to allow food, medicines and other essential goods to be moved around the country as normal. But lorry-owners had to get permits from the strikers before they could transport food and drugs freely. The lorries and vans had to show a sign, like the Boots van in this picture.

PICKETS Any lorry without a permit and a notice was likely to be stopped by the strikers. They set up pickets – groups of striking workers – outside factories, docks and other work-places. The pickets' job was to explain their strike, and try to stop strikebreakers going into work. This picture shows pickets on duty outside the London Docks.

DEMONSTRATIONS The strikers held demonstrations during the strike to keep their spirits up and win support. Here is a parade in Manchester. You can see a banner, and a brass band.

VIOLENCE   Most of the picketing was quite peaceful. But a few incidents led to fighting with the police. This picture shows a crowd of strikers and bystanders stopping a van in London's East End. You can see the date on the cinema poster — Monday May 10th.

SABOTAGE In some places, buses and trains were smashed up by the strikers. Usually it was because volunteers had been driving them to help break the strike. Some buses, vans and trains were set on fire, others were overturned or stoned.

One incident did nearly cost lives, however. It happened near Newcastle where strikers had removed a section of railway track to derail the express train, the *Flying Scotsman*. The strikers had warned the volunteer driver, but he insisted on driving on, and the train was derailed. No one was killed but several passengers were taken to hospital.

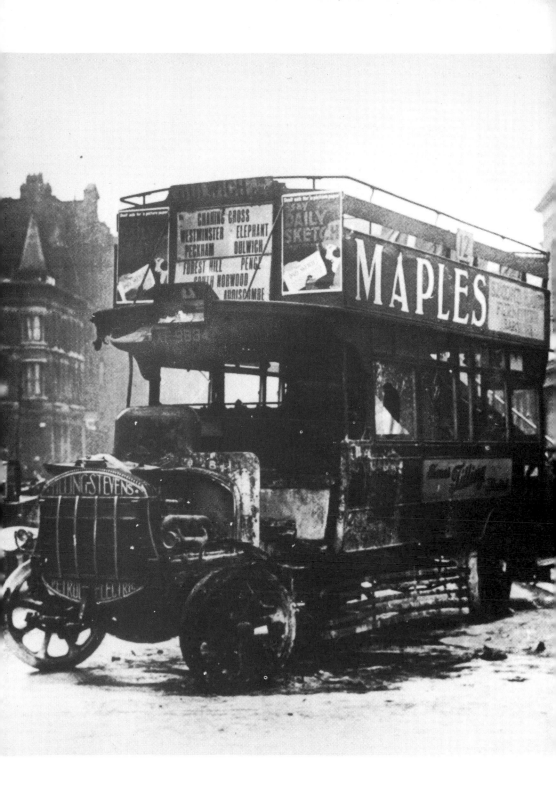

STRIKERS' FAMILIES Life was tough for many strikers' families during the strike. Few unions had enough money to pay much strike pay. There were no state benefits for strikers, though some strikers got 'Poor Law Relief' — a small sum of money paid out of the rates. The children in the picture above are scrounging for bits of coal at a big railway station in London.

POLICE VERSUS STRIKERS Apart from a few street battles, the strikers got on quite well with the police. Most strikers wanted the police to prevent

violence. In Plymouth, the Chief Constable organized a football match between the police and the strikers. The Chief Constable's wife kicked off; the strikers won 2 −1.

PASSING THE TIME This crowd of strikers is watching a broken-down bus being towed away. The streets were full of men with no work to do. Some

strikers held marches, others held brass band con-
certs. In Plymouth there was a church service for
strikers.

THE DAILY MIRROR
£5000 FOR A DERBY FORECAST

1 CIRCULAR ROUTE 1
EALING B^DY TO EALING B^DY
VIA
NOTTING HILL GATE
ALDWYCH
KENSINGTON CHURCH

THE DAILY MIRROR
£5000 FOR A DERBY FORECAST

"BLACK & WHITE"

LF 9379

4 The Strike-breakers

Many people had a lot of sympathy for the miners. But most people were against other unions joining the strike in support of the miners. They saw a General Strike as an attack on the way Britain was run, and feared it might lead to a revolution like the one in Russia in 1917, when the workers overthrew the Tsar and established a communist state.

The T.U.C. tried hard to persuade people that it was not a 'political' strike like that. The Government tried to persuade them that it was. Winston Churchill, who was Chancellor of the Exchequer, started a Government newspaper called the *British Gazette*: it set out to show that the strikers were against the rule of law. The usual newspapers did not appear, so it was hard to find out what was happening. By 1926 some families had a wireless, and the BBC was the main source of news. The Government tried to control what the BBC said about the strike, but the BBC insisted on reporting what it thought right.

Thousands of volunteers came forward to do the strikers' jobs. They were mainly middle-class people, and some strikers resented well-off people helping to break their strike which was largely about low pay. However, the volunteers probably had very little effect in keeping things going. The picture shows volunteers driving a London bus. Some volunteers became 'Special Constables' and helped the regular police keep order. However, the people who really broke the strike were not the volunteers, but the 'blacklegs' – people who went on doing their jobs as normal.

THE ARMY The Army was called out at the start of the strike, but stayed mainly in the background in camps outside the big towns. The picture shows troops of the Scots Guards arriving in Hyde Park, London. They guarded trains, food vans and buses. In a few places, they marched through towns as a show of strength to warn the strikers against violence. Sailors helped to run power stations.

FOOD CONVOYS In London the Army brought armoured cars to guard convoys of food lorries. The strikers had stopped food being moved out of the docks. So the Government got volunteers to unload the food from the ships, and the Army guarded the convoys of lorries that carried it from the docks to be sent all over London. As you can see, very few police were needed to control the crowd.

MILK SUPPLIES Milk was an essential supply and had to be kept moving. It would not keep, as there were no refrigerated lorries then. Hyde Park was made the centre of milk supplies. Thousands of lorries with milk churns came in from the country, and volunteers helped to send the milk out to all parts of London.

REGULAR POLICE The police guarded buses, factories and docks and kept an eye on the strikers' pickets. These mounted police have drawn their batons after riots at the Elephant and Castle in London.

SPECIAL CONSTABLES Many thousands of 'Special Constables' were recruited. These were volunteers taken on just while the strike lasted. You can see them collecting their truncheons and armbands in the picture. In some towns, the strikers themselves were taken on as specials to keep order. But in most places the specials were disliked by the strikers. They were often jeered at and pushed around.

VOLUNTEERS SIGN ON Some people had signed on as volunteers with the OMS — the Organisation for the Maintenance of Supplies — before the strike. Now thousands more followed. In London they queued in the courtyard at the Foreign Office, waiting to sign on. Similar scenes took place in other big towns.

THE PLUS-FOUR BRIGADE Most volunteers were middle-class people. Although they helped to keep things moving, they were not always very good at the jobs they took on. Wearing their fashionable 'plus-four' trousers tucked into their socks, they were

laughed at by the strikers. They often had to cover the engines with barbed wire to prevent strikers from disabling the vehicles. The picture shows cheering strike-breakers who have just passed their bus driving tests.

STUDENT VOLUNTEERS This picture shows students unloading cargo from a ship's hold at the docks. Many college students volunteered as strike-breakers

— driving trains and buses, working in the docks and
doing many other jobs. Most students were eager to
volunteer as strike-breakers.

TRANSPORT VOLUNTEERS One of the volunteers' favourite jobs was driving buses, lorries, or better still tramcars. Often there was a policeman on guard. Here barbed wire is being draped over the front of a bus to stop strikers getting at the engine. Notice the plus-four trousers again.

PLAYING TRAINS This picture shows a volunteer at work in a signal box. He is obviously enjoying himself! The chance to drive trains was exciting, but the volunteers had little idea how to do it. Very few trains ran. Even so, four people were killed in collisions, and many engines were damaged.

WOMEN VOLUNTEERS   Women volunteers played their part too. A few drove lorries, like the one opposite. Society ladies ran canteens for the volunteers in the London parks. They felt they were doing their bit for Britain. They were often working for the first time in their lives.

KEEPING IN TOUCH Most of the newspapers were hit by the strike. Some brought out typewritten broadsheets like the copy of *The Times* opposite. People gathered outside newspaper offices, newsagents and other shops to read the news pinned up outside. The Government brought out its own newspaper — the *British Gazette* shown opposite. The paper was run by Winston Churchill who was violently against the strikers.

The British Gazette

Published by His Majesty's Stationery Office.

No. 3.   LONDON, THURSDAY, MAY 6, 1926.   ONE PENNY.

NATION CALM AND CONFIDENT

Gradual Recommencement of the Railway Services.

GOOD FUEL AND FOOD SUPPLIES.

Volunteers In Large Numbers At All The Centres.

OFFICIAL COMMUNIQUE

FOREIGN VIEWS OF THE STRIKE.

THE WAY OF PANTIES.

Paris Press.

"ORGANISED MENACE."

The Real India Behind the General Strike.

Red River Bill Open.

T.U.C. FLOUTED

Hospital without Electricity

WORK DISORGANISED

Operating Theatres Closed

YORKSHIRE INCIDENTS

NOTICE TO PRINTING TRADE.

MESSAGE FROM THE PRIME MINISTER

STANLEY BALDWIN.

CHANNEL SERVICES   **FOOD SUPPLY NORMAL.**

The Times

No. 44263   London Wednesday, May 5, 1926.   Price 2d

WEATHER FORECAST. Wind N.E.; fair to dull; risk of rain.

THE GENERAL STRIKE.

A wide response was made yesterday throughout the country to the call of those Unions which had been ordered by the T.U.C. to bring out their members. Railway workers stopped generally, though at Hull railway clerks are reported to have resumed duty, confining themselves to their ordinary work, and protested against the strike. Commercial road transport was only partially suspended. In London the tramways and L.G.O.C. services were stopped. The printing industry is practically at a standstill, but lithographers have not been withdrawn, and compositors in London have not received instructions to strike. Large numbers of building operatives, other than those working on housing, came out. The situation in the engineering trades was confused; men in some districts stopped while in others they continued at work. There was no interference with new construction in the shipbuilding yards, but in one or two districts some of the men engaged on repair work joined in the strike with the dockers.

N. Derbyshire and Monmouthshire.

Evening papers appeared at Bristol, Southampton, several Lancashire towns and Edinburgh, and typescript issues at Manchester, Birmingham and Aberdeen.

The Atlantic Fleet did not sail on its summer cruise at Portsmouth yesterday. The men went on shore duty.

Road and Rail Transport - There was no railway passenger transport in London yesterday except a few suburban trains. Every available form of transport was used. A few independent omnibuses were running, but by the evening the railway companies, except the District and Tubes, had an improvised service.

Among the railway services to-day will be 6.30 a.m. Manchester to Marylebone; 6.30 a.m. Marylebone to Manchester; 10.10 a.m. Marylebone to Newcastle; 9 a.m. Norwich to London; 9 a.m. King's Cross to York; 3 p.m. King's Cross to Peterborough; 9 p.m. Peterborough to King's Cross. L.M.S. Electric trains will maintain a 40 minutes service. On all sections of the Metropolitan Railway except Moorgate to Finsbury Park, a good service will run to-day from 6.40 a.m.

BLACKLEGS This picture shows non-striking lorry drivers, playing a game while they wait for orders. The Government promised to protect men who defied their union. The poster opposite shows Baldwin's promise. For years after, men who had refused to strike were called blacklegs. Probably less than a quarter of all working men were on strike.

TO ALL WORKERS IN ALL TRADES

ADDITIONAL GUARANTEES

Official

Every man who does his duty by the Country and remains at work or returns to work during the present crisis will be protected by the State from loss of Trade Union benefits, superannuation allowances or pensions. His Majesty's Government will take whatever steps are necessary in Parliament or otherwise for this purpose.

STANLEY BALDWIN.

H.M. STATIONERY OFFICE.

GETTING TO WORK Not a lot of normal work was done during the strike, but people did try to get to work all the same. They crowded into lorries, and people with cars put up signs offering lifts. Here you can see how some people got to work — even in a steam lorry, or in the back of a van.

76

5 Back to Work – and After

Early in the strike, talks between the Government and the T.U.C. began to try to end it. Sir Herbert Samuel worked out a plan with the T.U.C. to get the miners back to work. The miners would have to agree to a cut in wages, in return for changes in the way the coal industry was run. The miners refused to accept wage cuts, but the T.U.C. decided to withdraw their support from the miners, and called the strike off on 12th May. The strike had lasted only nine days.

Apart from the miners, the strikers went back to work. The Government thanked the volunteers for standing by their country in time of need. In the mining areas things got worse for the miners. The owners still refused to take them back without a cut, and in July the Government passed an Act adding an hour to the miners' working day. Slowly the miners drifted back to work, even with lower wages and longer hours. They had to. Otherwise they and their families would have starved. By November all the miners were back at work. The General Strike had failed totally.

Poverty and unemployment got worse over the next few years. It was called the 'Great Depression', or the 'Slump'. At one time nearly 3 million workers had no jobs. Workers like the one in the picture could be seen standing aimlessly on street corners wondering whether they would ever work again. Ten years after the General Strike there were still hunger marches of jobless men seeking help. In 1939 Britain was back at war – with Hitler's Germany.

SAMUEL RETURNS FROM ITALY Sir Herbert Samuel came back from Italy to help bring an end to the strike. He sailed into Dover, and the racing driver, Sir Henry Segrave, met him and rushed him up to

London. This picture shows Segrave in his Sunbeam.
Samuel spent days talking to the T.U.C. about a deal
to end the strike. Segrave went on to win the world
land speed record in the Sunbeam.

THE STRIKE CALLED OFF The T.U.C. thought the Government had promised to deal fairly with the miners, and make the owners agree to Samuel's terms. So they called the strike off. The picture above shows the T.U.C. leaders coming back to their London headquarters after telling the Prime Minister it was over. Opposite Winston Churchill's wife, Clementine, says 'Well done' to the Prime Minister, Stanley Baldwin, in Downing Street.

THANKS TO THE VOLUNTEERS The volunteers and strike-breakers were warmly thanked. Below is a certificate of thanks to a volunteer bus-driver, for coming to the support of the Country in a serious crisis.

WE DESIRE on behalf of His Majesty's Government to thank you in common with all others who came forward so readily during the crisis and gave their services to the Country in the capacity of Special Constables.

Stanley Baldwin
PRIME MINISTER.

W Joynson Hicks
HOME SECRETARY.

Downing Street,
May, 1926.

To *A. J. Burleigh*
METROPOLITAN SPECIAL CONSTABULARY RESERVE.

BACK TO WORK   And so it was back to work — for some. This picture shows railway workers waiting to start work again at the end of the strike. But many employers punished the strikers: some employers would only allow the men to return to work if they took lower pay, or agreed to leave their trade union. At first the strikers thought they had at least won a fair deal for the miners. But the miners got nothing: they stayed out.

BACK TO NORMAL? Life returned to normal for most people after the strike. Above you can see society people at the Ascot Races in June 1926 – just a few weeks after the strike. Opposite is a picture at Epsom Races the same month: a miners' band is playing to collect money for miners' families. Life was far from 'back to normal' for them.

THE MINERS DRIFT BACK TO WORK The miners did not get their 'fair deal'. The owners still demanded wage cuts and longer hours, and offered nothing in return. Many miners' families were now in real poverty. Families lived on bread; children fell ill from lack of proper food, and many went barefoot. Collections were made to help them, and soup kitchens were set up. The miners' strike began to crumble. Rather than see their families starve, the miners began to drift back to work in September and October — on the owners' terms. Here you can see miners going back in the Midlands — defeated.

DEFEAT FOR THE MINERS At last the miners' union had to accept defeat. In November 1926 a conference was held in London. The picture above shows A. J. Cook, outside the conference hall, talking to reporters. It was Cook who said 'Not a penny off the pay, not a second on the day'. He had to accept them both — and nothing in return.

THE GREAT DEPRESSION Times were to get still worse. In 1929 the great crash on America's Wall Street stock exchange led to poverty for millions — not just in America, but all over the world. Britain suffered throughout the 1930s. Hunger marches were

held to demand jobs and support. The unemployed marched from as far north as Scotland to London to persuade the Government to help them. The picture above shows one famous march — the Jarrow Crusade from Durham to London in 1936.

STREET FIGHTING   The General Strike had failed so totally that people did not want to try it again. In the 1930s, poverty and depression led to street fighting instead. In Germany, Italy and other countries, the Nazis and fascists were in power. The British fascists – Sir Oswald Mosley's Blackshirts – rioted in the streets. Police here are breaking down a fascist barricade in London's East End in 1936.

BACK TO WAR It was poverty and unemployment in Germany after the First World War that brought Hitler to power in 1933. While Britain had hunger marches and fascist riots in the 1930s, Germany was re-arming. Britain was still slowly recovering from the Great Depression when the Second World War broke out in 1939. Strikers and their sons went to war side by side with volunteers and their sons.

New Words

Blacklegs — a striker's term for workers who continue to work during a strike

Despatch rider — a motorcyclist who carries messages

General election — the choosing of representatives to form a new Parliament

Hunger march — protest demonstration or procession of the unemployed

Labour Exchange — government agency which finds work for the unemployed, pays out unemployment benefit, etc.

Lock-out — the closing of a work-place by employers to make employees agree to something

Pickets — group of striking workers who stand outside their work-place to persuade non-striking workers not to go into work

State benefit — sum of money, or other form of aid, given to the needy by the Government

Strike — to stop work as a protest against working conditions, low pay, etc. A *general strike* is a strike of all workers in different trades intended to bring the country to a standstill

Strike pay	money paid to workers from trade union funds during a strike
Trade union	group of workers of the same trade who join together to bargain with employers for better pay and working conditions
Trades Union Congress	the organization which joins together all the larger unions in Britain

More Books

Nine Days in May by Patrick Renshaw (Eyre Methuen Picturefile, 1975)

The General Strike by R. J. Cootes (Longman, 1964)

The Twenties by R. J. Unstead (Macdonald Educational, 1973)

The General Strike: A Collection of Contemporary Documents (Jackdaw Publications, 1972)

Britain between the World Wars by Marion Yass (Wayland, 1975)

Date Chart

11th Nov 1918	End of the First World War
14th Dec 1918	Election returns Lloyd George to power
1919	Police and rail strike
1920	National coal strike
1921	Government hands running of mines back to mine-owners
	Miners' lock-out
	'Black Friday' — failure of proposed miners' strike.
1924	Britain's first Labour Government under Ramsey Macdonald
1925	'Red Friday' — Government gives mine-owners a grant to delay cut in miners' wages. Threatened coal strike called off
March 1926	Samuel Commission publishes its report on the Coal Industry. Wage cuts proposed
3rd May 1926	General Strike begins
12th May 1926	T.U.C. calls General Strike off. Workers, except miners, return to work
July 1926	Act passed to add extra hour to miners' working day
Sept—Oct 1926	Miners drift back to work
1929	Wall Street crash
1930s	Great Depression with riots and hunger marches
1936	Jarrow hunger march to London
3rd Sept 1939	Britain and France declare war on Germany. Beginning of the Second World War

Index

Picture acknowledgements

BBC Hulton Picture Library 11, 13, 14, 15, 16–17, 18, 20–21, 24, 25, 31, 50, 51, 52–3, 54, 56, 57, 59, 61, 62–3, 64–5, 66, 67, 68, 69, 70, 71, 72, 74, 75, 76, 78–9, 83, 84, 85, 86, 87, 88–9, 90, 91; John Topham Picture Library 29, 36, 42–3, 58; Mansell Collection 12, 26; Mary Evans Picture Library *jacket picture;* National Museum of Labour History 22, 23, 30, 40, 44, 45, 46, 47, 49, 60, 82; Popperfoto 10; T.U.C. Library *frontispiece,* 6, 19, 28, 32, 34, 36–7, 41, 73. The remaining pictures are from the Wayland Picture Library.